Foreword

For some time I have had the privilege of meeting each week at the Poetry Studio with a group of exceptional and gifted poets. They share a passion for poetry and an unabashed determination for close reading and self critique. It is remarkable to me the range and brilliance they bring to their writing. This anthology brings together a sample of their poems.

Where Edward Barker's poems let us explore paradoxes at the outer edges or beyond the borders of lived experience, Judy Brown's are unanswerable, physical poems with ideas brought to existence in them. Matthew Brown works with poetry's form and music, and is often focused on memory or incident or place, whether real or imagined. Beatrice Garland writes about being a particular person, with a particular view of being alive – with the limiting case of facing death – in a world of connectedness with others. Susan Grindley shares poignant experiences with the reader which can make them laugh out loud or shed an inner tear, often at the same time. Alex Humes' wild and thought-provoking poems are concerned with the space between subjective, egoic conflicts and wider, reified ones. Valerie Josephs

intently everywhere she goes; this provides much of her inspiration. In her series of prose poems she is the flâneuse in London and Paris. June Lausch is interested in an intensified focus on an idea or image, sticking with it, taking it as far as she can, often blurring the edges of concrete and abstract. Barbara Marsh's direct and startling poems expand the personal standpoint to explore the 'once-removed' (step-relationships, in-laws, etc) and, spreading outward, she also allows a fictional character to dictate poems to her. Stuart McKenzie looks for the pure potentiality of the now. He does this through the simple act of writing, forensically focusing on the mundane and everyday. Rose Rouse is involved, through writing, in exploring her relationship with others and the world. She strives for and achieves a stark emotional honesty blended with a wry look at existence and the cracks that let the light in. In his often baroque and always entertaining poetry Simon Rees-Roberts tries to make sense of the day-to-day in an increasingly incomprehensible world.

All that said, the one true way to garner an appropriately lively appreciation of the work of these tremendously varied and delightful poets is to read it. Their work is bold and beautiful. I leave you with it and to its enjoyment.

John Stammers

Contents

Helena Paleologina

When her empire lay in ruins,
 cupolas rubble,
 and she could no longer
command the seas
to lay down their waves,
 she took to knitting
 with twine of angel's-guts
 steeped in milk of Belladonna;
 the vestments so luminous
 their wearers were placed
at sunset upon parapets
to guide or warn poets
into the arms of Byzantium.

Helena Paleologina Weaving

A sparrow flew
through the open casement.
She caught it in one movement
of her sceptre hand,
and though it had never known
what it is to be cupped by a palm,
the sparrow did not struggle.

The Caliphs' Janissaries
had by now breached the outer walls,
and were impaling martyrs along the watch towers.

The Empress felt that miniature
beating of a living heart,
and it was more than any counterpoint
to her, who had heard
the choirs of Chrysostom
melt snow on Mount Olympos
and the descant of Magus the Castrato
too sad for flesh.

How it reminded her
of the heartbeat of the sea
booming along the headlands
of her girlhood.
Startled, she looked
the sparrow in the eye again,
desiring to trace the origin
of that thought,
but only God's indifference stared back.

Edward Barker

Where to Begin a New Life

Perhaps at this border, where my skin's seal
docks with the wet air and where mosquitoes
patrol, nipping and puckered up to get in.

Fifteen years ago, my legs flowered
into blisters of body-filtered water. Now
my connective tissue flows slowly back

through time until I understand where
I am. The place knew: I was a returner,
had borrowed some of its diesel-perfumed air

for my own signature blurt of pheromones,
eaten yard-long beans grown from a feed
of night-soil, had drunk imported wine,

cool and costed as the nights started to thin.
It's coming back: how I started where
you're starting now, in an empty flat, glass-

floored with new varnish. I know how the sun
comes misty-sly over the painted hills. By
eleven I'd beg for fog at the curtainless blaze.

The thermostats are set to absolute zero;
we still shed moisture. Just watch it rise
into a sweat of saltwater pearls on our chests.

The Dehumidifier

The air grows wetter by the hour: my breath
adds to the exhale of the soil-banked wall.
While I'm gone you'll suck it dry. Your humming
motor runs the downing of a hundred pints;
night and day, inhuman lungfuls pass across
your plastic gills. How the rest works I can't tell.

Perhaps you harm the air so much it cedes
its dampish gift without a fight. But I'd prefer it
if somewhere in your workings bracken uncrinkles,
and, above, on cool-touch branches, wetness
gathers, like a troupe of sea-monkeys taking rest.
A seeker might find peace inside your frost-caves
as moisture ripens, fruits and falls into the pooling jug.

By Friday, it's the usual story: your green light bleats
red: you've drunk your fill. I click out the reservoir
and pour away the absent week's wet harvest
wasting what you worked so hard to build.
Once more I will myself to neither cry nor sweat:
hereafter I may live as aridly as decency permits.

Judy Brown

Guts

Weigh it first in the palm of your left, belly up.
Then flop flank down on the block, tail fanned out
against marble or oak. Note the gold scales,

the red-eye dots. See the gills collapse,
the arsehole's dark O. Touch your blade tip here,
clip a nick, press till the slit grows. Grip.

Use a rag if you must, then slice through chest
to throat – a fine line where pale flesh thins.
Stop before the slack jaw's wishbone. Make it clean.

Fishwives, it's said, could cut through fifty
a minute, their blunt fingers stunk to old age.
Slide yours between the flaps to catch

the guts, a moist purseful of soft mechanics.
This is what there is: a tube for in and out
made slime. Snip the gullet, tug

the slick innards till membrane peels
from bone. Adjust your hold, thumb
back muscle, let the knife-point pierce

the spinal column. Ooze as black as claret dregs.
Most goes with a running tap; some spots
need an edge, a fingernail. With luck, what's found

between the ribs is pink. Leave the head,
let eyes pearl in the pan, skin butter-crisp
with sting of lemon and dill. What's left

is skeleton: skull, vertebrae, fin; tail, a tattered
flag on a grounded ship. Fold the waste
in old news, seal the lid from night's predators.

Brass

Voice gone, he used a bell,
an old clanking bedside thing
made of brass. He'd ring
for help with all

the simple tasks that failed
him: food, dress, piss.
She'd come from corners in the house
to smooth the sheets, bale

the pot before it spilled.
His mouth open for the spoon;
she held his look, the room
quiet now at last, still.

Matthew Brown

...while everything else remains the same

We met before email, before texting,
when living happened at a walking pace.
Sometimes telephones were answered
or sometimes not, left to ring
all afternoon in sunlit anterooms,
dust suspended in the parallelograms.
That was when the mystery of absence
might fill the air for days and silences
could be themselves, unfathomed.
When the weather grew warm
a message scribbled on an envelope
might be forgotten in the pocket of a coat.
Land-lines could go wrong and wires
get crossed, a private conversation overheard,
or posted letters might arrive too late:
a crumpled envelope returned weeks later
marked in blue: *not known at this address.*
Yet marriages were made, babies delivered,
anniversaries noted or forgotten – for still
the world is everything that is the case.

Hotel

The room is scarcely larger than the bed.
How do we take this step, from here to there?

Do we fall upon each other as we are
or take our clothes off first, like every day?

I'm shaking with excitement, fear and cold.
I could suggest we both go home, but

I don't know if I'd mean it; nor would you.
Instead I wait. You brought me here. Now show

me what to do. The linen is unruffled, white.
I like the way you touch me, as if you were

thinking about the shapes, the entrances you
come across: my body rises from the deep,

borne on the wave that's stirred up by your hands
to meet your more-than-readiness. And then

this feeling I'd forgotten, this surprise,
this finding out that what gets made is love.

Beatrice Garland

From a Bus Passing Through Victoria Park on a Morning in October

The park is a Chinese landscape painting.
The middle ground has risen in white mist
above the foreground where small trees
and railings are inked black.

The lake, the bridge and the pagoda,
which would have added much,
are painted on the reverse of the scroll.
Tower blocks stand in for mountains.

Next stop, I'm getting off the bus.
By the time it pulls away
I shall have disappeared in my grey coat.
Look for my red shoes half way up the picture.

Home from Hospital

Anything purple or yellow had to go,
anything unfinished or beyond repair.
In the pastel hospital I had made plans
for all the things that didn't measure up.
The orange chair must be re-covered,
the chipped, red filing cabinet repainted,
ivy in the garden cut right back.
I tore my diaries into confetti,
gave clothes I'd never mend to charity
and sold books I had never opened.
I can't watch television, it's too loud,
too bright. Mornings I don't speak,
sit on my own in my white dressing-gown
listening to Scarlatti one note at a time.

Susan Grindley

Another Aspect to Inter-Species Love Affairs

It doesn't matter what the killer whale is doing in my room.
What's important is that we're listening to fireworks,
me lying east to west across his tailfin.

The smell of gunpowder gets me thinking of the holiday
we took to the lakes with a French girl
who carried him everywhere.

All whales need to be carried sometimes, he says,
and I don't argue. I don't like to forget he's no ordinary whale:
I'm a killer, he once said, *in the same way you're sapiens.*

During a lull in the fireworks I ask him
if he's ever dreamt of moving off to warmer waters,
somewhere perfect, thick with fish.

All water is perfect water, he says,
carefully sets me on my feet, and with a quick
flick of his tailfin breaks both my legs.

Carnival Neptune

It's 2 am and we're up on the aft deck.
You started crying when I called you unique.
I swill the blue neon light into our brandy.
Look, I say, *a shooting star* and you cry more.

Behind us the captain in babygrow and medallion.
Drunk, he opens a white roll like a book
and buries his nose right up to the hilt.
The pussy, he said, when Sam served him

cold eggs, *the little pussy hole have got no god.*
And we used this all morning till we'd used it up.
He stares at you hooked stiff over the gunwale
raises his eyebrows and touches his breasts.

I must have laughed because you turn around.
Captain, I say, *the ship is moving.* But you're long
gone and all at once there's an ocean in my room.
At four knots, he says, then sits down, eats bread.

Alex Humes

My Husband's Chair

I wasn't sure about moving it into my bedroom,
in case its presence might be too dominant,
as though it would be an inhibition.
On the contrary, it's a benign presence and I perch
on it, on the frame, to put on my tights and shoes.

This antique chair you used to sit on
at the partners' desk, to write your scores,
has an upright cane back and the top of the frame,
the cresting, is carved in low relief with what look
like walnuts, which could be the wood it's made of.

I've decided to leave the chair the way it is.
Once the caners used to call at the door to ask
if you had anything to repair and they would weave
outside, as they brought the replacement cane on their bikes
and the price would depend on the number of holes.

Two Poems after Tu Fu (712 – 770)

Recording My Thoughts While Travelling at Night

A sea of hard seats in bright light,
large steel birds roost on runways,
stars punctuate the darkening sky.
The departure boards are ruthless.
How could departure times be so wrong?
I quit my perch due to boredom and rage,
wander aimlessly into duty-free,
a solitary traveller between there and here.

Visitors Have Come

Though they are late, they are always welcome.
I too am late, I have not yet started to cook
our supper. Earlier I chose four fillets of trout;
they looked so fresh and pink. I'll serve them
with jasmine rice, soy sauce and fresh ginger.
I wish I hadn't forgotten the bok choi.
I like it when friends sit in the kitchen and wait
for food and we all help to finish the wine.

Valerie Josephs

Three New Potatoes

It started about a year ago,
your spare keys discovered in a tin.
I'd watch you leave then let myself in,
take your coffee cup from the sink,
still warm, and sip the dregs,
or press a finger on loose crumbs
and settle back in your easy chair.

In time I wanted more: nail clippings,
a hair from your comb, stubble, fluff,
this dust composed of human skin.
Breathe into towels to find your smell,
re-arrange them perpendicular to the rail.
I'd sort, fold, tidy, smooth and plump
and find a pair for each unmatched sock.
It was never enough.

Three new potatoes from a bag in your fridge.
Float them in water, watch them boil,
bounce, bubble in their baby-brown skins.

Some Words Fly, Some Don't

The word became flesh and hovered above us,
started to soar, tried with all it had to gain height
but then fell, like a bird shot out of the sky
and landed with a small thud onto the kitchen table,
where it lay with its dead weight between us,
while we sat, face to face, unable to speak,
until you gave it a prod, edged it towards me.
I watched the smear of blood as it formed a trail
and I pushed it back.

June Lausch

Mr Ferndean dreams through New Year's Eve

May Woerner rings his front doorbell.
He has the title – *Sounds of the Front Bell,* the colours
straight out of Douglas Sirk. Golden Reggie starts barking
until Mr Ferndean gives him the favoured blue plimsoll –
    tooth-marked
rubber receding, sole full of holes – and the dog, mouth full,
makes a sound more akin to singing, tail furiously sweeping
the coffee table, the low ebony bench in the entry hall.
Mr F straightens his tie – the green-flecked woollen one –
and approaches the door. Reggie sings.

Mr Ferndean opens the front door. May stands
in a flowered cotton shift, her bare arms illuminated
in the early evening sun. Then, as always, Reggie drops the shoe;
tail knocking the large vase-cum-umbrella stand askew,
he licks May Woerner's knees, puts his paws on her thighs,
and, his lucky muzzle now near her left breast,
slobbers along the embroidery at the décolletage. It takes
much of Mr Ferndean's strength to pull the dog off.
He apologises to May, offers to pay for the drycleaning.

Mr F opens his eyes. The sun is bleeding into the room.
Reggie stands by the bed, tail on automatic. Mr Ferndean glares
at his dog, pushes the covers off and steps into his slippers.

Monday

As you open the door to your day
you say *she'll get better.* Your voice
is all bounce; you liken recovery
to a car needing a service, our lives
will be like they were before,
the doctors will pull out the splinters,
your daughter will come back. I am not sure.
I know you are saying this because
it's all you can do.
Yes, I say. *Yes.*

Barbara Marsh

Hairbrush

Our histories have been escaping us.
Check all the data mingling
in those abandoned strands of hair.
Eager genome sequences
willing to spill the beans
on an everyday still life.
Like the Inuk Man
will I be resurrected in 5000 years,
(well, in a pencil drawing at least)
balding with shovel-shaped teeth
sporting a 1970s style feathercut
after my frozen locks are found?
O hairbrush! O harbourer of DNA!
A diary of every complaint,
strand after strand
documenting you were half way
between this and that.
Look no further than this hairbrush –
evidence of spoilt lives
clings to its fine bristles.

Now Voyager

Further than the reach of '77
you are here, unmanned –

beyond the lip of all planets:
the well of connected worlds,

acquiring before another
the status, soon-to-be-star,

placed between the luminous –
sail thou forth to seek and find.

Stuart McKenzie

Ingredients

Contains
Infrequent discriminatory language and behaviour.

Contains
Scenes of sexual violence, flash photography and traces of nuts.

Contains
Strong horror, Liquorice Allsorts, woodlice,
reference to onanism, sciatica and inflatable penises.

Contains
E 102, harpies, methylisothiazolinone,
peat-free compost, low level radioactive waste,
occult blood, Allura red and Curcumin.

Contains
The last trump and Whore of Babylon in radiance,
roads liable to subsidence, psychoanalysis,
outdated risk-assessment, flatulence
and minds scalded by the ooze of yesteryear.

Contains
All possibilities pounded to dust and reduced
to the size of the angels' dance floor,
frozen laughter and gravitational collapse,
a singularity: the beginning, crushed into a tiny fist.

On Hungerford Bridge

His Spanish guitar is missing three strings
and his mouth several teeth, there's a rip on his cheek.
A wisp of grey hair has escaped his pony-tail
and aspires to be silk in the faltering breeze.
He sits with his instrument upright and thumps it,
(think of Picasso, the early blue period)
– schitzo furioso with random twangs.
The song's beyond rap, it's a vile fulmination.

Behind him two Witnesses hand out their brochures,
their smiles have gelled – guaranteed to endure.
The strap-line is something like *why go on living?*
There's reason enough when the world's full of busking
and so far there's always been a tomorrow.
Put a pound on for God in this lunatic's hat.

Simon Rees-Roberts

The Meaning of Space

Inside are the rudimentary items:
local butter, Himalayan pink salt, tamari,
no siege-mentality tins and jars,
luxury is limited to one packet of fig rolls.
His concept of capaciousness is alien.
My symptoms are clear:
staccato intakes of breath,
a feeling of mild nausea,
light stabbing pains in the heart.
Cupboard envy is the prognosis.
I reflect briefly on emptiness.

La Tempête

Napoleon planted these pines,
the soil is sandy but not a beach.
I want to lie down,
stare upwards like a child
who hasn't had enough clouds.
The watery landscape keeps me upright.
On cherche les oiseaux,
mais on n'entend que les chants.
The sky deceives itself.
We talk (my French friends and I)
about how to inhabit the truth,
to sink our teeth into ice-cream
without fear of incrimination or shame.
We sit with gratitude on a fallen trunk,
taste different sorts of apples,
note the sour and sweet preponderances.

There is an ending amid a swamp,
my descent into deep water is fast,
tears escape, there is a tempestuousness
to their interminability. I am scared.
My friends, my parents become.
This vulnerability is unmapped.

Rose Rouse

The Group

Edward Barker has been involved in The Group since 2004. He has published poems in various magazines, including McSweeney's and Poetry Review and has won prizes or commendations at the Ledbury, Wenlock, Essex and National Poetry Competition, as well as being short-listed three times for the Bridport. He is included in the Forward Poems of the Decade 2011 anthology.

Judy Brown's first collection, Loudness (Seren, 2011) was shortlisted for the Forward/Felix Dennis and Fenton Aldeburgh first collection prizes. She was Poet in Residence at the Wordsworth Trust for 2013 and a Gladstone's Library Writer in Residence in 2014. Her latest pamphlet is One of the Summer People (WT, 2013). She joined The Group in 2009.

Matthew Brown is a freelance journalist and writer. His poems have appeared in a number of publications, including Magma, Other Poetry and South Bank Poetry. He grew up in Durham, lives in east London and has been in The Group for six months.

Beatrice Garland works in the National Health Service as clinician, teacher and researcher in psychological medicine. She has been in The Group since February 2013. In the same year she published her first collection, The Invention of Fireworks, which has been short-listed for the Best First Collection in the Forward Prizes.

Susan Grindley is a founder member of The Group. She has had poems highly commended in the Philip Larkin and the Edwin Morgan poetry competitions and has read at the Ledbury Poetry Festival and the Edinburgh Book Festival. Her pamphlet, New Reader was published in 2013 by Rack Press.

Alex Humes read Russian at university and has since worked as an actor and teacher. He has been a member of The Group for about 3 years. He lives in Brixton where he is an assistant beekeeper to his neighbours' colony.

Valerie Josephs was born in London. She has been in The Group for eleven years. Magazines: Brand, Magma, Painted, Spoken and Smiths Knoll. Anthologies: Gobby Deegan's Riposte (Donut Press), Solitaire and Buzz (Templar Poetry), Said and Done (Brittle Star), I am Twenty People (Enitharmon), Images of Women (Arrowhead), Virago Book of Christmas and Birdbook 11 (Sidekick Books). A visual artist, she studied in Chicago, London and Glasgow.

June Lausch is a teacher and lives in Stoke Newington. She has been published in magazines, including Magma and South Bank Poetry. She was a runner-up (twice) in the Troubadour Annual Poetry Competition. In 2010 she was commissioned by The Whitechapel Art Gallery, to write poems inspired by the work of Alice Neel. She has been a member of The Group for several years.

American-born **Barbara Marsh's** first collection To the Boneyard (Eyewear Publishing) came out in 2013. As a singer/songwriter/musician, she was one-half of cult band The Dear Janes, releasing three albums across Europe and the U.S. A member of The Group for ten years, she lives and teaches in London.

Stuart McKenzie is a freelance fashion illustrator, living and working in London. He joined The Group this year. His poems have appeared in Magma, Envoi, South Bank Poetry, Urthona, The Delinquent, Domestic Cherry, The Interpreter's House, AnOther Magazine and PLU magazine. He is the author of Creative Fashion Illustration (published by Bloomsbury in 2014).

Simon Rees-Roberts joined The Group ten years ago but vanished for most of the decade. Recently he returned to scowl at mainly familiar faces. His poetry has appeared in Magma, Poetry London, Still, Carapace and other magazines. Resident of the leafy suburbs, he divides his time between writing, drawing, cooking, cycling and searching for lost equipment.

Rose Rouse is a writer, journalist and PR. She has been in The Group since 2010. Her poems have appeared in Magma and South Bank Poetry. Her non-fiction book, A London Safari: walking adventures in NW10 (Amberley Publishing) is out in October 2014.